Maggie

Enjoy!!

Caroline

Bees, Butterflies and Blossoms

of Southern Arizona

Volume 1

Ann

Bees, Butterflies and Blossoms

of Southern Arizona

Volume 1

A

Celebration of Southern Arizona Image Gallery

by Murray Bolesta

CactusHuggers Publishing

ISBN-13: 978-0-9797842-0-0

Book designed by Murray and Agnès Bolesta

Special thanks to Sandy McMahan

Published in the U.S.A. in 2007 by CactusHuggers Publishing, P.O. Box 1501, Green Valley, Az., 85622, 1-520-207-8452, www.CactusHuggers.com

Preface

As my second "Celebration of Southern Arizona Image Gallery," Bees, Butterflies and Blossoms of Southern Arizona represents a more microscopic view of this borderlands region than does Moods of the Santa Ritas of Southern Arizona. But my overall sentiment is the same: I want to show the elemental beauty of this place to impress the urgent need to preserve open spaces in this area, and to save the wild living things that need this diverse habitat.

The abundance of life forms that live or visit here do so because of the greatly varying elevations in this part of the Sonoran desert, from the low desert scrub at 2,500 feet, to the 8,000+ foot levels of the mixed conifer forest. Moreover, the domain of this book is at the confluence of the immense Sonoran, Chihuahuan, and Sierra Madre bio-regions, multiplying the species here.

This region, encompassing the open spaces of Santa Cruz, Cochise, and southern Pima counties, is in peril. The relentless march of urban development diminishes the natural, rural, and cultural heritage of borderlands Arizona. The people of this state are now becoming more committed to saving this heritage. I dedicate these pages to the visitors, newcomers and longtime residents who take action to preserve those things which make this region unique.

Almost all of these photographs were taken in the wild, or otherwise in uncontrolled circumstances. I visited no botanical garden, arboretum, or zoo. Further, the plants and creatures in these pictures are mostly commonplace. While the book's title describes its main contents, other subjects were sometimes used to add texture.

This book is not formally structured; instead the images are grouped by a subjective perception of colors which gradually merge into one another. Primary hues – red, blue and yellow, and secondary colors – orange, tan, green, purple, pink and magenta – provide an organizational principle for the sequence of images. If to us the colors of flowers are a big part of their attraction, to pollinators, such as bees and butterflies, the shades of a blossom tell about the quality of the nourishment it offers. The photo subjects are often tiny spots of vivid color in a vast and often pallid earthen landscape.

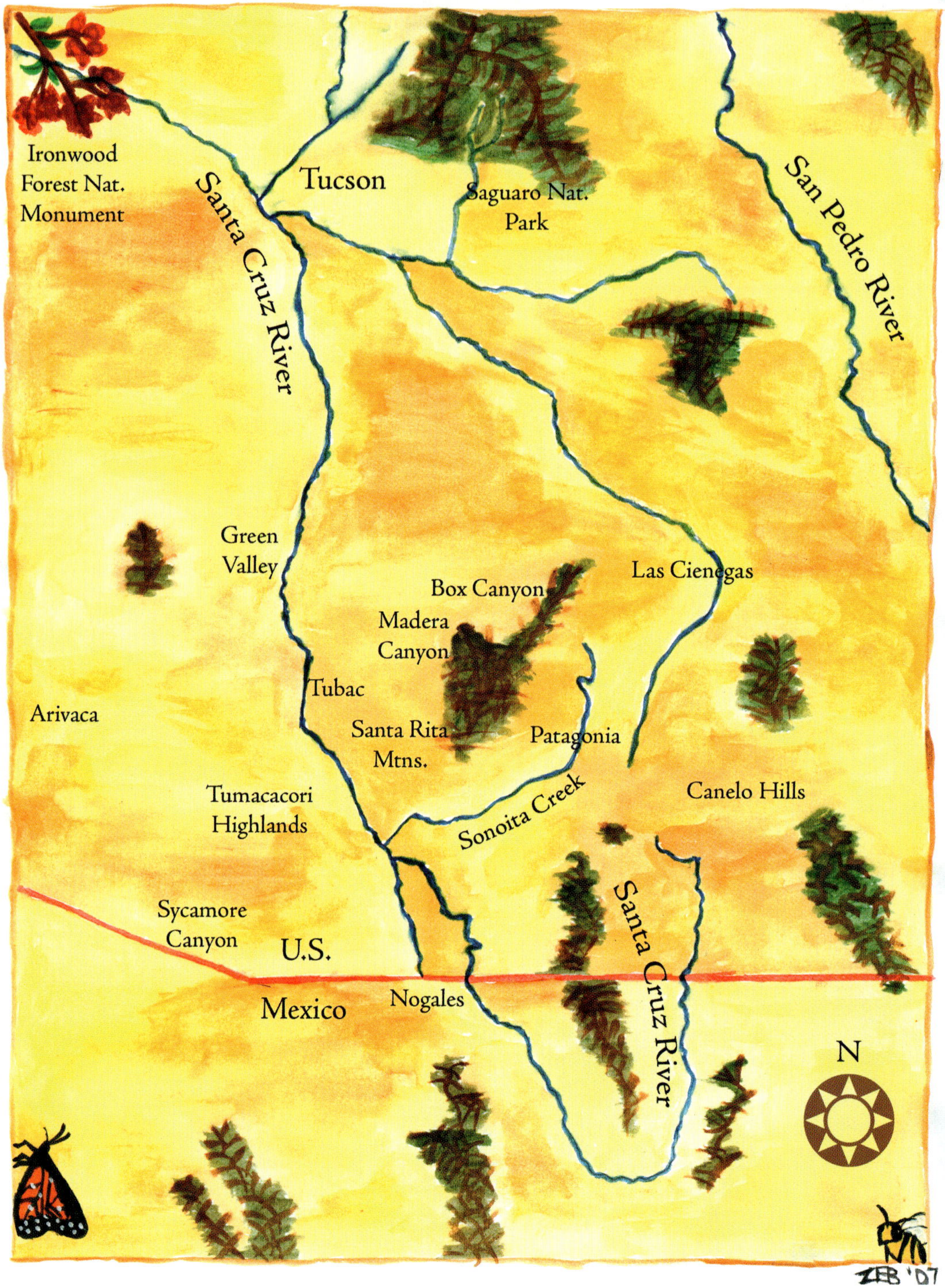

This area, as drawn by our daughter Zoé.

Water

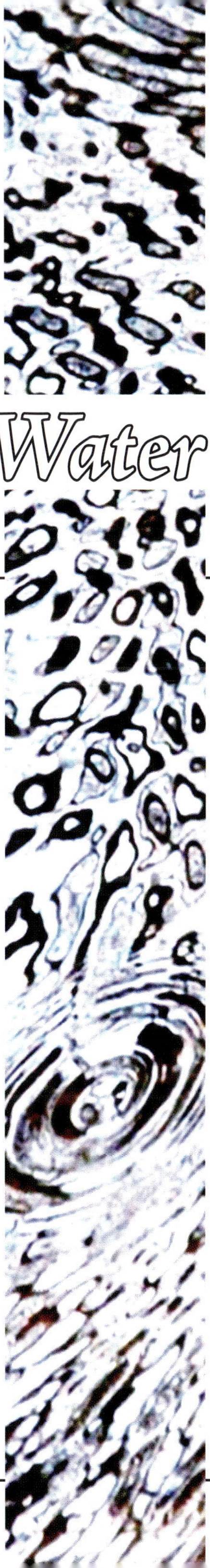

Southern Arizona's precious, fragile spring waters are the lifeblood of many of this book's images. They give birth to the hue and substance of the area's natural beauty.

A vestige of their earlier forms, southern Arizona's spring waters often sink into the parched ground within a short distance of their surface origin. But these tiny and charming wild waters of Arizona continue to sustain vibrant wild life, enchanting those who discover these hidden spots.

Empire Gulch spring water, Empire Ranch, Las Cienegas National Conservation Area, Sonoita, February.
A reflection of purity is the spirit of this image.

Willow and cottonwood leaves, Canelo Hills Cienega, Sonoita, November.
These fallen leaves represent the classic southern Arizona Fremont cottonwood-Goodding's willow gallery forest.

Viceroy butterfly, San Pedro River area, April.
Resting near the water of a secret side canyon of the lower San Pedro River, this mimic of the Monarch has the tell-tale black line across its hind wings.

Sycamore Canyon, May.
A fallen log straddles the creek in the famous and fabulous Sycamore Canyon of the Pajarita Wilderness, a few rugged miles from the Mexican border.

Reds

The color red provokes and incites. Its emotional impact has been used by humans to stir political and economic responses profitable to the purveyor. Nature's supposed guilelessness is brought into question with red.

Barrel cactus, Green Valley, August.
The second-springtime rains of the so-called monsoon season add a wondrous luster to southern Arizona, and a break in the heat, which usually peaks in June before the storms arrive.

Claret Cup cactus, Sycamore Canyon, April.

This blossoming specimen, growing on the rocky canyon slopes, radiates its color vividly against the grey of its surroundings.

Dragonfly, Sycamore Canyon, November.
This graceful creature flittered over the creek, then rested long enough to show off for a picture.

Cardinal flower and Mexican Yellow butterflies, Sycamore Canyon, November.
Taken just a few moments before the previous picture of the dragonfly, this photo shows just a portion of the clustering butterflies.

Bee and Buckhorn cholla, Green Valley, May.
Spotting and capturing the fleeting and delicate hues hidden inside a harsh landscape is part of the fun of living in southern Arizona.

Ocotillo, Ironwood Forest National Monument, April.
This little bee is dwarfed by the towering, swaying branches of an iconic Sonoran plant blooming at its peak.

Mexican Bird of Paradise, Barrio Viejo, Tucson, July.
Also called Red Bird of Paradise, this flowering shrub is a popular southern Arizona urban garden decoration. A hot summer late afternoon captures its silhouette here.

Empress Leilia butterfly, Madera Canyon Wash, September.
This brilliant little creature, resting on granite, is a bit more than an inch wide, with wings outstretched.

Barrel Cactus buds, Green Valley, August.
About to open, these buds perhaps need coaxing from a little more monsoon rain in the heavy clouds overhead.

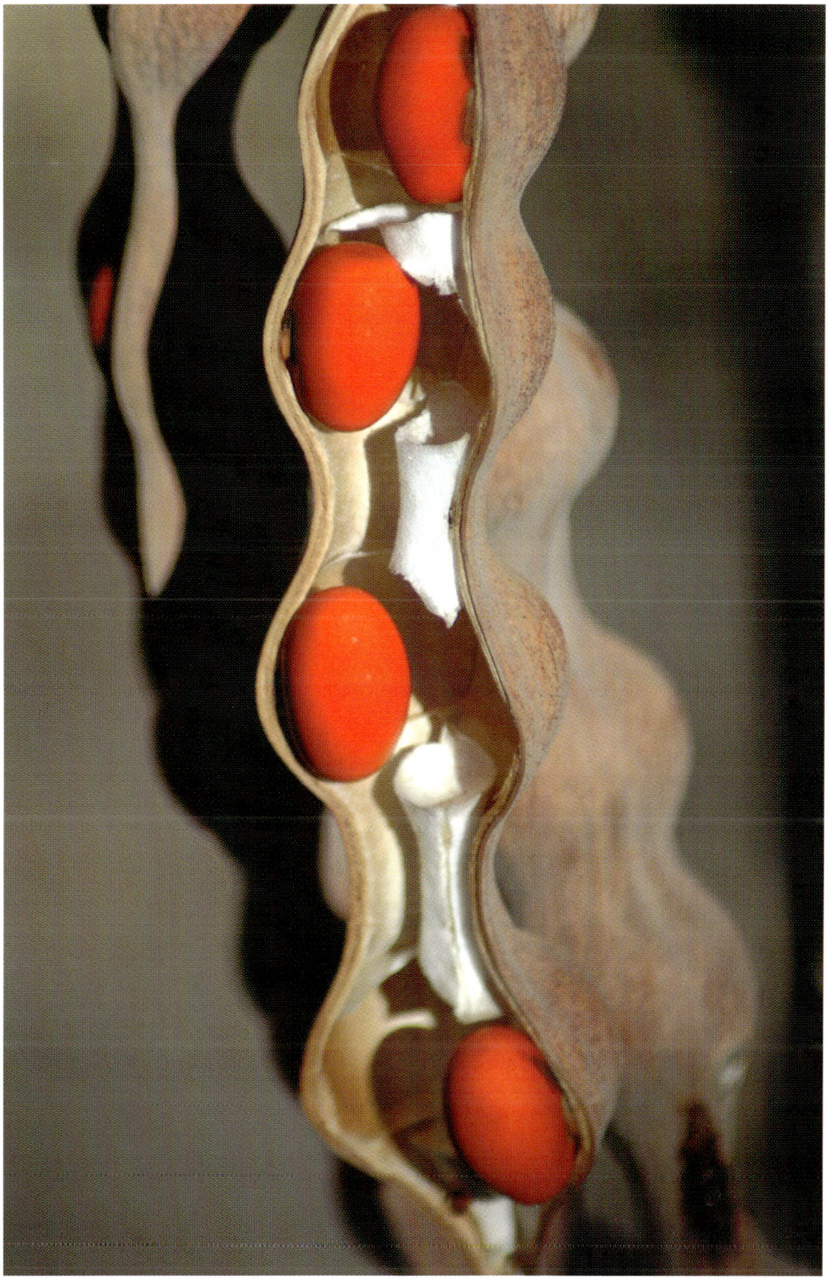

Coral Bean pod, Agua Caliente Canyon, Santa Rita Mountains, November.
Finding color in November can sometimes be a challenge in southern Arizona, but I succeeded with this intriguing abstract.

Dragonfly, Canelo Hills Cienega, Sonoita, July.
Clinging to a twig on a nice warm morning, this creature rests just over a creek.

Prickly Pear cactus, Saguaro National Park East, April.

A Sonoran icon, the blossoms in this picture show the different hues of their life cycle, and can be numerous enough at this time of year to surround the desert hiker.

Arizona Poppy, Box Canyon, August.
Favorable weather brings out these beauties to carpet many acres of higher desert area.

Mexican Yellow butterfly, Madera Canyon Wash, October.
This month is glorious for butterflies of all persuasions in the Madera area.

Barrel Cactus fruit, Green Valley, January.
I think these cute shapes resemble little plastic pineapples.

Manzanita, Cochise Stronghold, September.

East of the San Pedro River, the legendary Apache leader Cochise is said to be buried beneath the trees of Dragoon mountains.

Pineapple cactus, Green Valley, July.

A relatively scarce cactus in southern Arizona, this plant's blossoms have a subtle hue and sit atop a shape reminiscent of the cactus' namesake.

Pineapple cactus, Green Valley, July.
Another view of this small cactus pits its size against the immensity of southern Arizona's monsoon skies.

Cattails, Arivaca Cienega, January.
Where cattails thrive, water is nearby.

Queen butterfly, Sycamore Canyon, November.
A long camera lens softens the scene behind this common but striking creature.

Yellows

Shades of yellow are similar in many of southern Arizona's flowering plants, from poppies to palo verde. The bane of botanists, many area blossoms, or 'darned yellow composites', can look alike.

Crab spider on Brittlebush, Peck Canyon, Tumacacori Highlands, August.
Can you see the spider in this picture? Many cannot without a second glance. This creature changes colors to blend with its host plant, making it very hard to spot, which, I'm sure, is nature's point.

Yellow columbine, Sycamore Canyon, April.
Columbine is a graceful and plentiful addition to Sycamore canyon during this month, adding swaths of color to the creek banks.

Striped Cucumber beetle and squash blossom, Canelo Hills Cienega, Sonoita, July.
A good picture is created by this little creature's contrast with the plant's vivid hues.

Tombstone rose (Lady Banks rose), Tubac, April.
A wooden fence is adorned in the spring, adding more charm to a street of this artist community.

Palo Verde, Green Valley, April.
These trees are a widespread partner to the mesquite and the ironwood tree in the Sonoran desert, but unlike the other two, produce a riot of yellow this month.

Wild sunflower, Arivaca Cienega, September.
Birds from this wetland park find the seeds from this plant to be a favorite.

Tarantula Hawk wasps on Milkweed, Canelo Hills Cienega, July.
These creatures, with colorful wings and fanciful antennae, can have a sting worse than a bee, I'm told.

Sycamore bark, Madera Canyon, June.
While neither a bee, a butterfly, nor a blossom, this bark illustrates southern Arizona's diversity of natural textures.

Cattails, Sycamore Canyon, July.
The reeds are seen again here, this time in another place, from another angle and with different light, projecting a different hue.

Tiny Checkerspot butterfly, Madera Canyon Wash, September.
A cloudy day casts no shadow beneath this miniscule creature, less than an inch wide, with outstretched wings.

Blues

The color blue often denotes a cooler tone, but in Southern Arizona blue is most commonly seen surrounding an un-mellow blazing sun.

Bougainvillea, Mission San Xavier del Bac, Tucson, June.
While not exactly native to southern Arizona, this blossom accents the distincive shapes and colors of the sky and edifice above it.

Spanish Dagger yucca and commercial airship, Tucson, April.
Here are blossoms at their peak and a blimp at its height.

Silverleaf Nightshade, San Pedro River, November.
No matter how much color this berried plant adds to a field, it's an example of the many invasive species that plague southern Arizona.

Exotic cacti and succulents, Tucson, April.

Decorative plants from deserts around the world are popular additions to the gardens of southern Arizona. The skyscraper in the background is a 10-foot wall downtown.

Saguaro cactus, Saguaro National Park East, May.

A round ball coming out of a Saguaro, sprouting blossoms, is the beginning of an arm. But with extremely slow growth, sometimes a round ball seems to stay a round ball.

Pipevine Swallowtail butterfly, Patagonia-Sonoita Creek Preserve, Patagonia, June.
This is an elegant pose for this common southern Arizona creature, creating a graceful image of unadorned wild nature.

Bluedick, Saguaro National Park East, February.

An early season show-off in the desert, this wildflower seems to burst towards the camera from the soil after a rain.

Morning Glory, Madera Canyon Wash, September.
The right moisture also brings out this carpet of blue, punctuated by an albino.

Santa Rita Prickly Pear cactus, Green Valley, April.
Heart-shaped new growth appears a few months late for Valentine's day.

Thistle, San Pedro River area, April.
This unidentified insect isn't exactly a bee, but the creature installed itself squarely in the middle of this blazing thistle, so I'm bringing him along.

Pincushion cactus, Green Valley, July.
A stamen projects from the blossom of this cactus cluster.

Rainbow cactus, Green Valley, May.

This relatively rare small cactus points its blossoms toward the spring sky for only a couple of days per year.

Staghorn cholla, Green Valley, April.
A decorative sprinkle of pollen coats these vibrant petals.

Rainbow cactus, Green Valley, May.
A bee bathes in pollen from this gorgeous blossom.

White

Pristine white, as the combination of all spectral colors, echoes the purity of unencumbered desert habitat struggling to remain pure.

Datura, Box Canyon, Santa Rita Mountains, August.
Commonly seen along southern Arizona roadways, this large specimen gladly welcomes a monsoon shower

Desert Chicory, Saguaro National Park East, Tucson, February.
A shadowless image benefiting from an overcast sky, this wildflower makes an early season appearance when the moisture is just right.

Variegated Fritillary and Tarantula Hawk wasp, Canelo Hills Cienega, Sonoita, July.
Little can be said to embellish this elegant image of unfettered nature inside the rarest of southern Arizona's habitats, a riparian marshland.

Prickly Poppy, San Pedro River area, May.
No matter how weedy the rest of this plant can appear, its large blossoms are always a bright and welcome sight.

Horizons

The hard task of preserving open spaces in southern Arizona involves more than maintaining the trackless desert vistas that are a large part of the popular image of this region.

While those unfettered landscapes replenish one's soul and provide places for human recreation, their key feature is the vital habitat for the wild plants and animals of this area.

Further, the agricultural connection with the land that gave birth to this nation requires the vistas to remain open.

Southern Arizona's human horizons are connected directly with its physical horizons.

Soaptree yucca, San Pedro River area, June.

Bending from its weight, this succulent punctuates the open spaces to the east, as the Sonoran desert transitions to the Chihuahuan.

Spent Sotol stalk, Tumacacori Highlands, March.
At day's end, some uncommon March clouds add drama to this wilderness scene.

Self Portrait, Saguaro National Park West, May.

*A*BOUT THE AUTHOR: *a relative newcomer to southern Arizona with a business background vastly unlike his new vocation, Murray Bolesta was inspired to reignite an old zeal for photography by the raw beauty and fragile diversity of borderlands southern Arizona. Further, he soon recognized the many threats to the natural, rural, and cultural heritage of southern Arizona, and formed CactusHuggers to support efforts to preserve open spaces. Murray lives in Green Valley with his wife Agnès.*